ARCTIC TERN MIGRATION

BY REBECCA HIRSCH

The Child's World®

Published by The Child's World®
1980 Lookout Drive • Mankato, MN 56003-1705
800-599-READ • www.childsworld.com

ACKNOWLEDGMENTS
The Child's World®: Mary Berendes, Publishing Director
Content Consultant: Dr. Tanya Dewey
   University of Michigan Museum of Zoology
The Design Lab: Design and production
Red Line Editorial: Editorial direction

PHOTO CREDITS
Neil Bradfield/Dreamstime, cover (bottom), 2-3; Igor Lovrinovic/
Dreamstime, cover (top), 1, back cover; Tony Brindley/Shutterstock Images,
4-5; The Design Lab, 6-7; Andrew Howe/iStockphoto, 8; Arto Hakola/
Shutterstock Images, 9, 10-11; Mike Morley/iStockphoto, 12; Gail Johnson/
Shutterstock Images, 13; Gail Johnson/Bigstock, 14; Harry Kolenbrander/
iStockphoto, 15; Uryadnikov Sergey/Shutterstock Images, 16-17; Fotolia,
18-19; iStockphoto, 20-21; Atlas Images/iStockphoto, 22-23; Pauline S
Mills/iStockphoto, 24-25; Horst Puschmann/iStockphoto, 26-27; Noah
Strycker/iStockphoto, 28

Design elements: Igor Lovrinovic/Dreamstime

ISBN 9781609736163
LCCN 2011940059

Printed in the United States of America

ABOUT THE AUTHOR: Rebecca Hirsch, PhD, is the author of several nonfiction books for children. A former biologist, she writes for children and young adults about science and the natural world. She lives with her husband and three daughters in State College, Pennsylvania.

TABLE OF CONTENTS

ARCTIC TERNS

Of migratory birds, Arctic terns are the long-distance champs. Each year these small birds fly from one end of the earth to the other. That flight takes them from the Arctic to the Antarctic. It is the longest migration of any animal on Earth.

The Arctic tern's lifetime journey is its migration. This is when an animal moves from one **habitat** to another. Migrations happen for many reasons. Some animals move to be in warmer weather where there is more food. There they can reproduce, or have their babies. And these migrations can be short distances, such as from a mountaintop to its valley. Or they can be long distances, like the flight of the Arctic tern.

Arctic terns fly all the way across the world during their migration.

MIGRATION MAP

Arctic terns nest all over the Arctic. The Arctic includes areas in North America, Iceland, Greenland, northern Europe, and Russia. Every year the terns fly south to the shores of Antarctica and back again. They have a **latitudinal** and **seasonal** migration.

Different Arctic terns fly along different routes. The routes depend on where they nest in the summer. Birds that live in western North America fly south along the Pacific coast. They follow the coast from Alaska and down North America. They keep going down to the tip of South America.

Birds that nest in eastern North America and Greenland fly across the Atlantic Ocean. They head toward Europe. There they join up with terns flying from Russia and Europe. All the birds fly south together. They soar along Africa's coast. The birds split into two groups during the journey. One group continues to fly south along the African coast. The others cross the Atlantic Ocean and follow the coast of South America.

PACIFIC
OCEAN

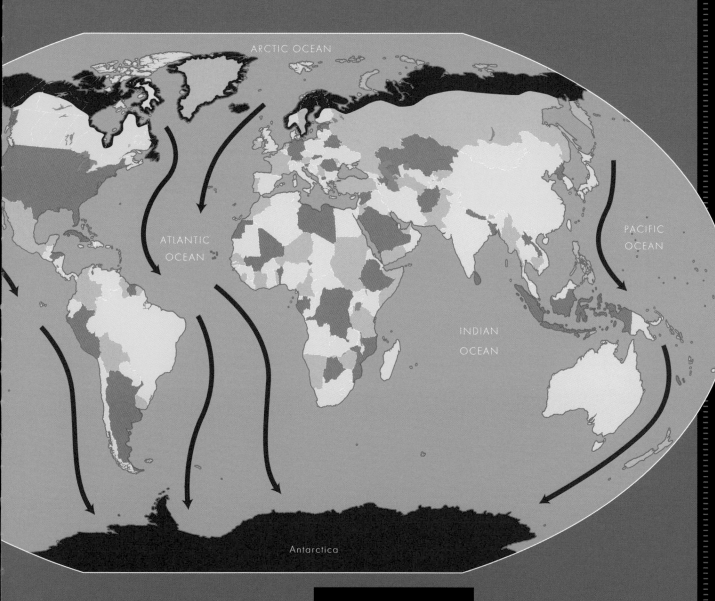

ARCTIC OCEAN

ATLANTIC
OCEAN

PACIFIC
OCEAN

INDIAN

OCEAN

Antarctica

Breeding Grounds

Wintering Grounds

LIFE OVER THE WATER

Arctic terns are birds that each weigh about the same as a lime. They are white and gray with black heads. Their beaks, feet, and legs are bright red or orange. They have long wings and a forked tail.

Arctic terns spend much of their lives in the air. They mostly fly over the open sea, far from shore. They come ashore only to breed. Like all flying birds, Arctic terns have a smooth shape. It helps them coast through the air. They have hollow bones. This makes them light. Their long and pointed wings help them fly long distances.

The light, slender bodies of Arctic terns are perfect for life in the air.

Arctic terns feed on small fish, crab, shrimp, and **krill**. The birds pluck food out of the sea. They also catch flying insects. When fishing, the bird beats its wings fast. It hovers above the water. Then it dives down into the water and catches a fish just under the surface.

Arctic terns are graceful and fast in the air. But, they are slow on land. They have very short legs. It looks like the bird is bending over when it stands.

Arctic terns are not good swimmers. Their webbed feet are too tiny to paddle water. The birds dive under the waves for fish, but they are only in the water for a short time. Then they are back in the air. The Arctic tern is a bird suited for life over the water.

Arctic terns quickly dive into the water to catch fish.

LIKE HUMMINGBIRDS, ARCTIC TERNS CAN HOVER IN THE AIR. THE TERN BEATS ITS WINGS AND STAYS IN ONE PLACE IN THE AIR. IT IS ONE OF THE FEW BIRDS THAT CAN DO THIS.

*An Arctic tern chooses
a mate, and the pair
stays together for life.*

10

BREEDING AND NESTING

Summer in the Arctic is short and full of life. The long, hard winter has passed. The ice and snow have melted. The frozen **tundra** thaws. The land fills with marshes and streams. The sun shines day and night.

In May, the Arctic terns arrive. They are ready to choose a mate. To court, first the female chases the male. Then the male performs a "fish flight." With a fish in his mouth, he chases, screams, and flies low over the female. He offers her the fish. If she takes notice, she will join him in flight. Once a male and female have paired, they stay together for life.

The birds nest together in large **colonies**. The nests are usually on rocky or sandy beaches. The beaches are out in the open, not in grassy areas. Each pair makes its nest on the ground. The nest is just a small area where the ground has been scraped away. Sometimes the birds line their nests with pebbles or sea grass.

The female bird lays one, two, or three eggs. Then both parents take turns sitting on the nest. They wait for the chicks to break out of their shells. The new chicks are wet at first. But soon they are dry. When they can move, the chicks quickly leave the nest. They hide in

Arctic tern nests are on the ground and in the open.

the brush. Their parents catch food and bring it to the chicks. The chicks grow quickly. After about three weeks, the young birds are ready to fly with the rest of the flock.

The tern's nest is open to attack from **predators**. Arctic foxes, rats, and skunks try to steal the eggs. Gulls and owls will also eat the eggs and the chicks.

Arctic terns do not nest in trees. Few trees grow where they live. They also do not nest in grassy areas. This may be because the birds' legs are so short. They may have trouble walking through tall grasses.

Chicks have speckled feathers that help them blend in with the rocky beach.

The birds do have ways to protect their young from predators. Parents cry loudly and dive at intruders. They peck them on their heads and backs. The brown speckled eggs have **camouflage**. They look like rocks. The chicks also have camouflage. Their tan and brown speckled feathers make them blend into their surroundings.

Arctic terns do not like their nests to be disturbed. They will dive at anyone who comes too close. Terns may also desert the eggs of a disturbed nest.

Arctic terns attack anything or anyone who gets too close to their nests.

PEOPLE KILLED TENS OF THOUSANDS OF ARCTIC TERNS AROUND THE TURN OF THE TWENTIETH CENTURY. THE FEATHERS WERE USED IN WOMEN'S HATS.

THE JOURNEY SOUTH

In August, life at the nesting grounds changes. The days grow shorter. Cold winds blow. The Arctic summer is ending. Arctic terns cannot survive the Arctic winter. The waters freeze. This makes it hard for the birds to find food. The Arctic terns migrate south to escape the cold.

As the summer days grow shorter, the birds gather in flocks. The flocks spend their days flying over the ocean. They fill up on food. They point themselves in the direction they are going to fly. From August to September, they begin their journey.

Terns fill up on food before their long flight.

The birds set off in the evening, just as the sun sets. The terns almost never rest on the journey. They fly on and on across the ocean. Sometimes they swoop low over the waves. If they spot fish, they dive in for a meal. The wind helps the terns fly. They fly in the same direction as the wind blows. The birds save energy so they can fly fast and far.

After several months, the birds end their journey. They have flown all the way to the opposite end of the earth. They arrive in October and November. Many end up on the shores of Antarctica. Some travel to the coast of Africa. And some go as far away as Australia and New Zealand.

During migration, terns dive into the ocean for food.

When the birds arrive, it is summer in the southern
habitat. The sun in the Antarctic shines day and night. Cool
breezes blow. The water is filled with krill and other food.

During this time, the birds molt. Their feathers fall out. The birds
may not be able to fly for a while. They rest on chunks of ice floating
in the sea. They wait for their new feathers to grow in. They get a new
set of feathers in time for the journey north.

Young Arctic terns do not migrate back to the Arctic right away.
They stay in the Antarctic for two years while they grow. Then they
will join the migration. They return to the Arctic to choose a mate, lay
eggs, and have chicks of their own.

Arctic terns enjoy two summers every year.

ARCTIC TERNS SOMETIMES STEAL FOOD FROM OTHER BIRDS. THEY DIVE AT THE BIRD. THIS SCARES THE BIRD AND IT DROPS ITS CATCH.

DURING THE ARCTIC AND ANTARCTIC SUMMERS, THE SUN NEVER SETS. THAT MEANS THE ARCTIC TERN PROBABLY SPENDS MORE TIME IN DAYLIGHT THAN ANY OTHER CREATURE ON EARTH.

BIRDS OF SUMMER

Arctic terns migrate from the earth's North to South Poles. They get to have two long summers each year. Seasons in the north and south are opposite. In the northern **hemisphere**, summer is in June, July, and August. During these same months, it is winter in the southern hemisphere. Later in the year, the seasons switch. During December, January, and February, the north has winter. And it is summer in the southern hemisphere.

By migrating so far, Arctic terns can feed in the rich polar oceans. They are filled with food to eat. The birds can live in the weather they choose. It is not too hot or too cold. And they can fly and raise their young in the long summer days filled with sunshine.

Arctic terns fly between Earth's poles.

TRACKING TERNS

Scientists who study birds knew Arctic terns flew from the Arctic to the Antarctic every year. But they were not sure exactly how far the birds flew in a year. They did not know the route the birds took. It is hard to watch a bird that spends most of its time flying far from land. To find out the distance they traveled, researchers put tiny devices on Arctic terns. These devices are about the size of safety pins and weigh less than a dime. Researchers caught terns in their northern habitat in Greenland and Iceland. They strapped the devices on the birds' legs and let them go. The scientists were able to track Arctic terns on their entire trip. The tracking device showed the route where the birds flew.

Scientists learned in 2010 that many terns start off across the Atlantic Ocean. But soon they pause in the north Atlantic Ocean. There the water has plenty of food to eat. The birds spend a month in this spot. It gives the birds fuel to continue the journey.

Scientists track terns to learn how far they fly.

Arctic terns fly many miles during their lifetimes.

The birds then continue on and fly all the way to Antarctica. On the return trip, the birds do not fly straight north. Instead they zigzag across the Atlantic Ocean. The birds probably choose this route because of the winds over the ocean. By flying with the winds, the birds save energy. This makes it easier to complete the trip.

The most amazing thing the scientists learned was how far the birds fly. Scientists had thought the birds made a yearly round trip of about 20,000 miles (32,000 km). But they learned the birds travel much further. Some fly as much as 50,000 miles (80,000 km) each year.

Over an Arctic tern's life, the miles add up. Terns can live to be more than 30 years old. One bird might travel 1.5 million miles (2.4 million km) in its life.

FINDING THEIR WAY

It is not known how Arctic terns find their way on such a long journey. Scientists think migratory birds probably use several methods. When flying at night, the birds may watch the stars and moon. Their spots in the sky may tell them where to go. By day, birds may use things on land to help them find their way.

Migratory birds may also use the sun as a compass. The sun moves across the sky during the day. Birds must know the time of day to follow the sun. When the birds want to fly south in the morning, they keep the sun on their left. To fly south in the afternoon, they keep the sun on their right.

Arctic terns may also be able to sense the earth's magnetic field. This is what makes the needle on a compass point north. Migrating birds have a magnetic matter inside them. It may help them sense Earth's magnetic field. The matter acts like a compass inside their bodies. It points them in the right direction.

Terns may use the
sun to decide which
direction to fly.

THREATS TO TERNS

Arctic tern nests are in danger from animal predators such as foxes and gulls. Another predator is people. In Greenland, Inuit people eat Arctic tern eggs. They have done this for many years. This may have caused the number of Arctic terns to fall. It is now illegal for people in Greenland to harvest Arctic tern eggs. But some people continue to take the eggs.

Today Arctic terns face another, even bigger challenge. All over the earth, the **climate** is warming. It is warming faster at the poles. The Arctic terns' summer and winter homes are changing fast. Scientists don't yet know how this change will hurt the birds. The birds may have to fly further to reach the habitat they need. Or the birds' food supply may fall.

It is important to know what may harm Arctic terns. People can work to help the birds. With care, Arctic terns will continue their mighty migration across the earth.

The Arctic tern faces threats from people and the climate on its migration.

TYPES OF MIGRATION

Different animals migrate for different reasons. Some move because of the climate. Some travel to find food or a mate. Here are the different types of animal migration:

Seasonal migration: This type of migration happens when the seasons change. Most animals migrate for this reason. Other types of migration, such as altitudinal and latitudinal, may also include seasonal migration.

Latitudinal migration: When animals travel north and south, it is called latitudinal migration. Doing so allows animals to change the climate where they live.

Altitudinal migration: This migration happens when animals move up and down mountains. In summer, animals can live higher on a mountain. During the cold winter, they move down to lower and warmer spots.

Reproductive migration: Sometimes animals move to have their babies. This migration may keep the babies safer when they are born. Or babies may need a certain habitat to live in after birth.

Nomadic migration: Animals may wander from place to place to find food in this type of migration.

Complete migration: This type of migration happens when animals are finished mating in an area. Then almost all of the animals leave the area. They may travel more than 15,000 miles (25,000 km) to spend winters in a warmer area.

Partial migration: When some, but not all, animals of one type move away from their mating area, it is partial migration. This is the most common type of migration.

Irruptive migration: This type of migration may happen one year, but not the next. It may include some or all of a type of animal. And the animal group may travel short or long distances.

> SOMETIMES ANIMALS NEVER COME BACK TO A PLACE WHERE THEY ONCE LIVED. THIS CAN HAPPEN WHEN HUMANS OR NATURE DESTROY THEIR HABITAT. FOOD, WATER, OR SHELTER MAY BECOME HARD TO FIND. OR A GROUP OF ANIMALS MAY BECOME TOO LARGE FOR AN AREA. THEN THEY MUST MOVE TO FIND FOOD.

GLOSSARY

camouflage (KAM-uh-flahzh): Camouflage is the coloring and markings that allow an animal to blend in with its surroundings. The tern's eggs have camouflage.

climate (KLYE-mit): The climate is the usual weather in a place. The tundra's climate warms in the summer.

colonies (KOL-uh-neez): Colonies are large groups of tern nests. Arctic terns nest in colonies.

habitat (HAB-uh-tat): A habitat is a place that has the food, water, and shelter an animal needs to survive. The summer tundra is the Arctic tern's habitat.

hemisphere (HEM-uhss-fihr): A hemisphere is one half of the earth. As it migrates, the Arctic tern flies to a different hemisphere.

krill (KRIL): A krill is a small animal that is like a shrimp. Arctic terns eat krill and other sea animals.

latitudinal (LAT-uh-tood-i-nul): Latitudinal relates to how far north and south something is from the equator. Arctic terns have a latitudinal migration route.

predators (PRED-uh-turs): Predators are animals that hunt and eat other animals. Gulls are predators of the terns' eggs.

seasonal (SEE-zuhn-uhl): Seasonal is something related to the seasons of the year. Arctic terns are seasonal migrating animals.

tundra (TUHN-druh): A cold area in northern North America, Europe, and Asia where no trees grow and the soil is frozen. The summer tundra is filled with food for terns.

FURTHER INFORMATION

Books

Catt, Thessaly. *Migrating with the Arctic Tern*. New York: PowerKids Press. 2011.

Lerner, Carol. *On the Wing: American Birds in Migration*. New York: HarperCollins. 2001.

Poyet, Guillaume, and Stephane Durand. *Winged Migration: The Junior Edition*. San Francisco: Seuil Chronicle: 2004.

Web Sites

Visit our Web site for links about Arctic tern migration: *childsworld.com/links*

Note to Parents, Teachers, and Librarians:
We routinely verify our Web links to make sure they are safe and active sites. So encourage your readers to check them out!

INDEX